TABLE OF CONTENTS

INTRODUCTION

Veganism is defined as a way of living that attempts to exclude all forms of animal exploitation and cruelty, whether for food, clothing or any other purpose.

For these reasons, the vegan diet is devoid of all animal products, including meat, eggs and dairy.

People choose to follow a vegan diet for various reasons.

These usually range from ethics to environmental concerns, but they can also stem from a desire to improve health..

Different Types of Vegan Diets

There are different varieties of vegan diets. The most common include:

Whole-food vegan diet: A diet based on a wide variety of whole plant foods such as fruits, vegetables, whole grains, legumes, nuts and seeds.

Raw-food vegan diet: A vegan diet based on raw fruits, vegetables, nuts, seeds or plant foods cooked at temperatures below 118°F (48°C)

80/10/10: The 80/10/10 diet is a raw-food vegan diet that limits fat-rich plants such as nuts and avocados and relies mainly on raw fruits and soft greens instead. Also referred to as the low-fat, raw-food vegan diet or fruitarian diet.

The starch solution: A low-fat, high-carb vegan diet similar to the

80/10/10 but that focuses on cooked starches like potatoes, rice and corn instead of fruit.

Raw till 4: A low-fat vegan diet inspired by the 80/10/10 and starch solution. Raw foods are consumed until 4 p.m., with the option of a cooked plant-based meal for dinner.

The thrive diet: The thrive diet is a raw-food vegan diet. Followers eat plant-based, whole foods that are raw or minimally cooked at low temperatures.

Junk-food vegan diet: A vegan diet lacking in whole plant foods that relies heavily on mock meats and cheeses, fries, vegan desserts and other heavily processed vegan foods.

Although several variations of the vegan diet exist, most scientific research rarely differentiates between different types of vegan diets.

VEGAN DIETS CAN HELP YOU LOSE WEIGHT

Vegans tend to be thinner and have a lower body mass index (BMI) than non-vegans

This might explain why an increasing number of people turn to vegan diets as a way to lose excess weight.

Part of the weight-related benefits vegans experience may be explained by factors other than diet. These may include healthier lifestyle choices, such as physical activity, and other health-related behaviors.

However, several randomized controlled studies, which control for these external factors, report that vegan diets are more effective for weight loss than the diets they are compared to

Interestingly, the weight loss advantage persists even when whole-food-based diets are used as control diets.

These include diets recommended by the American Dietetics Association (ADA), the American Heart Association (AHA) and the National Cholesterol Education Program (NCEP)

What's more, researchers generally report that participants on vegan diets lose more weight than those following calorie-restricted diets, even when they're allowed to eat until they feel full

The natural tendency to eat fewer calories on a vegan diet may be caused by a higher dietary fiber intake, which can make you feel fuller.

Vegan Diets, Blood Sugar and Type 2 Diabetes

Adopting a vegan diet may help keep your blood sugar in check and type 2 diabetes at bay.

Several studies show that vegans benefit from lower blood sugar levels, higher insulin sensitivity and up to a 78% lower risk of developing type 2 diabetes than non-vegans

In addition, vegan diets reportedly lower blood sugar levels in diabetics up to 2.4 times more than diets recommended by the ADA, AHA and NCEP Part of the advantage could be explained by the higher fiber intake, which may blunt the blood sugar response. A vegan diet's weight loss effects may further contribute to its ability to lower blood sugar levels

VEGAN DIETS AND HEART HEALTH

A vegan diet may help keep your heart healthy.

Observational studies report vegans may have up to a 75% lower risk of developing high blood pressure and 42% lower risk of dying from heart disease Randomized controlled studies — the gold standard in research — add to the evidence.

Several report that vegan diets are much more effective at reducing blood sugar, LDL and total cholesterol than diets they are compared to

These effects could be especially beneficial since reducing blood pressure, cholesterol and blood sugar may reduce heart disease risk by up to 46%

Other Health Benefits of Vegan Diets

Vegan diets are linked to an array of other health benefits, including benefits for:

Cancer risk: Vegans may benefit from a 15% lower risk of developing or dying from cancer (20Trusted Source).

Arthritis: Vegan diets seem particularly effective at reducing symptoms of arthritis such as pain, joint swelling and morning stiffness

Kidney function: Diabetics who substitute meat for plant protein may reduce their risk of poor kidney function

Alzheimer's disease: Observational studies show that aspects of the vegan diet may help reduce the risk of developing Alzheimer's disease

That said, keep in mind that most of the studies supporting these benefits are observational. This makes it difficult to determine whether the vegan diet directly caused the benefits.

Based Health Benefits of Eating Snacks Vegan

. A Vegan Diet Is Richer in Certain Nutrients

If you switch to a vegan diet from a typical Western diet, you'll eliminate meat and animal products.

This will inevitably lead you to rely more heavily on other foods. In the case of a whole-foods vegan diet, replacements take the form of whole grains, fruits, vegetables, beans, peas, nuts and seeds.

Since these foods make up a larger proportion of a vegan diet than a typical Western diet, they can contribute to a higher daily intake of certain beneficial nutrients.

For instance, several studies have reported that vegan diets tend to provide more fiber, antioxidants and beneficial plant compounds. They also appear to be richer in potassium, magnesium, folate and vitamins A, C and E

However, not all vegan diets are created equal.

For instance, poorly planned vegan diets may provide insufficient amounts of essential fatty acids, vitamin B12, iron, calcium, iodine or zinc

That's why it's important to stay away from nutrient-poor, fast-food vegan options. Instead, base your diet around nutrient-rich whole plants and fortified foods. You may also want to consider supplements like vitamin B12.

2. It Can Help You Lose Excess Weight

An increasing number of people are turning to plant-based diets in the hope of shedding excess weight.

This is perhaps for good reason.

Many observational studies show that vegans tend to be thinner and have lower body mass indexes (BMIs) than non-vegans

In addition, several randomized controlled studies — the gold standard in scientific research — report that vegan diets are more effective for weight loss than the diets they are compared

In one study, a vegan diet helped participants lose 9.3 lbs (4.2 kg) more than a control diet over an 18-week study period

Interestingly, participants on the vegan diet lost more weight than those who followed calorie-restricted diets, even when the vegan groups were allowed to eat until they felt full

What's more, a recent small study comparing the weight loss effects of five different diets concluded that vegetarian and vegan diets were just as well-accepted as semi-vegetarian and standard Western diets

Even when they weren't following their diets perfectly, the vegetarian and vegan groups still lost slightly more weight than those on a standard Western diet.

3. It Appears to Lower Blood Sugar Levels and Improve Kidney Function

Going vegan may also have benefits for type 2 diabetes and declining kidney function.

Indeed, vegans tend to have lower blood sugar levels, higher insulin sensitivity and up to a 50–78% lower risk of developing type 2 diabetes

Studies even report that vegan diets lower blood sugar levels in diabetics more than the diets from the American Diabetes Association (ADA), American Heart Association (AHA) and National Cholesterol Education Program (NCEP) In one study, 43% of participants following a vegan diet were able to reduce their dosage of blood-sugar-lowering medication, compared to only 26% in the group that followed an ADA-recommended diet

Other studies report that diabetics who substitute meat for plant protein may reduce their risk of poor kidney function

What's more, several studies report that a vegan diet may be able to provide complete relief of systemic distal polyneuropathy symptoms — a condition in diabetics that causes sharp, burning pain

4. A Vegan Diet May Protect Against Certain Cancers

According to the World Health Organization, about one-third of all cancers can be prevented by factors within your control, including diet.

For instance, eating legumes regularly may reduce your risk of colorectal cancer by about 9–18%

Research also suggests that eating at least seven portions of fresh fruits and vegetables per day may lower your risk of dying from cancer by up to 15%

Vegans generally eat considerably more legumes, fruit and vegetables than non-vegans. This may explain why a recent review of 96 studies found that vegans may benefit from a 15% lower risk of developing or dying from cancer

What's more, vegan diets generally contain more soy products, which may offer some protection against breast cancer

Avoiding certain animal products may also help reduce the risk of prostate, breast and colon cancers.

That may be because vegan diets are devoid of smoked or processed meats and meats cooked at high temperatures, which are thought to promote certain types of cancers

On the other hand, there is also evidence that dairy may help reduce the risk of other cancers, such as colorectal cancer. Therefore, it's likely that avoiding dairy is not the factor that lowers vegans' overall risk of cancer

It's important to note that these studies are observational in nature. They make it impossible to pinpoint the exact reason why vegans have a lower risk of cancer.

However, until researchers know more, it seems wise to focus on increasing the amount of fresh fruits, vegetables and legumes you eat each day while limiting your consumption of processed, smoked and overcooked meat.

5. It's Linked to a Lower Risk of Heart Disease

Eating fresh fruits, vegetables, legumes and fiber is linked to a lower risk of heart disease

All of these are generally eaten in large amounts in well-planned vegan diets.

Observational studies comparing vegans to vegetarians and the general population report that vegans may benefit from up to a 75% lower risk of developing high blood pressure

Vegans may also have up to a 42% lower risk of dying from heart disease

What's more, several randomized controlled studies report that vegan diets are much more effective at reducing blood sugar, LDL cholesterol and total cholesterol levels than the diets they are compared to

This may be particularly beneficial to heart health since reducing high blood pressure, cholesterol and blood sugar levels may reduce the risk of heart disease by as much as 46%

Compared to the general population, vegans also tend to consume more whole grains and nuts, both of which are good for your heart

6. A Vegan Diet Can Reduce Pain from Arthritis

A few studies have reported that a vegan diet has positive effects in people with different types of arthritis.

One study randomly assigned 40 arthritic participants to either continue eating their omnivorous diet or switch to a whole-food, plant-based vegan diet for 6 weeks.

Those on the vegan diet reported higher energy levels and better general functioning than those who didn't change their diet

Two other studies investigated the effects of a probiotic-rich, raw food vegan diet on symptoms of rheumatoid arthritis.

SNACKS VEGAN RECIPES

Homemade Vegan Mozzarella Sticks

Ingredients

Canola oil or oil of choice, for frying

1 package vegan mozzarella cheese (we used Miyoko's, see notes)

½ cup unsweetened almond milk

½ cup + 2 tablespoons all-purpose flour

½ teaspoon garlic powder

½ teaspoon onion powder

¼ teaspoon salt

⅛ teaspoon black pepper

½ cup bread crumbs* (see notes)

1 tablespoon of Italian seasoning

Homemade marinara sauce, for serving (optional)

Instructions

Preheat the oil in deep fryer to around 370 degrees.

Using a sharp knife, cut vegan mozzarella block in half long ways, and then into ½" strips. Set in fridge while preparing the batter.

In a medium bowl, add in the almond milk, 2 tablespoons of all-purpose flour, garlic powder, onion powder, salt, and pepper. Whisk together until all ingredients are well combined. Set aside.

In another medium bowl, add the bread crumbs and Italian seasoning. Whisk and set aside.

In a third bowl, add the remaining all-purpose flour and set aside.

Create a breading station: line up the bowl of almond milk batter, the bowl of all-purpose flour, and the bowl of bread crumbs.

Remove the vegan mozzarella from the refrigerator and set a large plate or baking sheet aside. Grab four forks. Use one set of the forks ("wet-forks") to pick up (do not pierce) one stick of mozzarella and submerge it completely in the batter. Shake off any excess and then drop it into the flour. Using the second set of forks (dry-forks), coat it completely in the flour. Pick up the stick using the "wet forks" and dunk it back into the batter, shaking off any excess. Drop the stick into the breadcrumb mixture and then using the "dry forks" generously coat it. Transfer the breaded stick onto the plate or baking sheet that you set aside and continue until you have coated all of the sticks. It is important to use the "wet forks" only for the batter and then the "dry forks" only for the flour and bread crumbs as this will prevent clumping and will also yield less of a mess.

Once all of the sticks are coated, line a plate with paper towel and set it aside. Pop the mozzarella sticks into the heated oil and fry them for 2-4 minutes, or until golden brown.

Once finished, transfer the mozzarella sticks to the paper towel-lined plate and allow them to cool until easy to handle.

Serve with marinara sauce and enjoy!

VEGAN COOKIE DOUGH

Ingredients

1 can white beans (rinse well)

2 tablespoons cashew butter

4 tablespoons maple syrup

1 teaspoon natural vanilla extract

2 tablespoons ground flax seeds

2 tablespoons almond milk

1 teaspoon hemp hearts

1/2 cup chocolate chips

Instructions

Place all of the ingredients except for the chocolate chips into a food processor.

Blend until smooth.

Add the chocolate chips and stir well with a spoon.

Serve with vegan cookies or fruit. If you want, you could add some vegan cookie crumbles on top.

DAIRY FREE CHEESE CRACKERS

Ingredients

1 cup flour (Use GF Measure for Measure if needed)

1/4 cup nutritional yeast

1/2 tsp baking powder

1/2 tsp garlic powder

1/4 tsp salt

1/4 tsp paprika

1/8 tsp turmeric

1 tbsp vegan butter

1 tbsp olive oil

1.5 tsp fresh lemon juice

4 tbsp water

olive oil spray

1/4 tsp course salt

1/2 tbsp Italian seasoning*

Instructions

1. Preheat oven to 350 °F.

In a bowl, combine flour, nutritional yeast, baking powder, garlic powder, salt, paprika, and turmeric.

Mix using a fork until combined.

Add in the vegan butter, olive oil, and lemon juice.

Mix again, using fork, until the dough and crumbly (about the consistency of a crumb topping).

Add the water a tablespoon at a time, mixing after each time until the dough is cohesive and forms a balls. *Could use your hands during this process if it helps.

Tear two pieces of parchment paper, large enough to fit a baking sheet.

Place dough ball in between the two pieces of parchment paper.

Roll out dough into a roughly 11×13 inch rectangle. *This does not need to be completely perfect

Remove top sheet of parchment paper and discard.

Use a pizza cutter make lines 1-2 inches apart vertically. And then repeat horizontally.

Using the small end of a skewer (wooden or metal), drive a small hole into the center of each cracker.

Place pachment paper with crackers onto baking sheet and spread out so they are not touching. *Crackers can be very close to each other but should have space to not be touching.

Spray lightly with olive oil

Top with course salt and Italian seasoning evenly.

Cook for 18-23 minutes or until golden brown.*

Remove and let cool. Keep in a sealed container.

VEGAN ONION RINGS

Ingredients

2 sweet onions

2/3 cup all-purpose flour

2/3 cup unsweetened almond milk

1 teaspoon garlic powder

1 teaspoon smoked paprika powder

1 tablespoon nutritional yeast

1/4 teaspoon salt

1 cup panko bread crumbs

Instructions

Combine the all-purpose flour, garlic powder, smoked paprika powder, nutritional yeast, salt, and unsweetened almond milk in a bowl and stir well.

Peel the onions and cut them into about 1/4 inch rings. Carefully separate the rings from each other.

Fill a bowl with panko flakes. Coat each onion ring in the flour spice mixture. Then coat it in the panko flakes afterwards.

Line a baking sheet with parchment paper and place the onion rings on top. Preheat the oven to 350 °F and bake them for 20 minutes. Flip them after 10 minutes.

Serve immediately with ketchup or dip of choice.

COCONUT AND PB SPICED ENERGY BITES

Ingredients

260 g smooth peanut butter

120 ml maple syrup

130 g whole rolled oats

100 g shredded coconut flakes

2 tsp mixed spice

Instructions

Place the peanut butter in a medium saucepan over a small heat and keep stirring until it's melted and runny. Add maple syrup and keep stirring to combine both, until you have super smooth consistency. Take off the heat.

In a medium bowl, mix together the oats, shredded coconut and mixed spice. Add to peanut butter and maple syrup mixture and combine all together. Using your hands (or a cookie dough scoop), roll the mixture between the palms of your hands into small balls and place on the baking tray lined up with parchment paper. Once you have used up all the mixture, place the tray with balls into the fridge for at least couple of hours. Enjoy!

Notes

Total time does not include chilling time

Feel free to use any type of your favourite spice

Energy bites will last for over a week in your fridge, just store them in the air-tight container.

VEGAN SPINACH ARTICHOKE DIP

Ingredients

1 cup white beans, rinsed and drained

1/2 cup cashews

1 tablespoon lemon juice

2 tablespoons nutritional yeast

1 onion, chopped

4 cups fresh spinach

2 cloves of garlic, minced

1 can artichoke hearts, drained and roughly chopped

salt

pepper

red pepper flakes (optional)

chopped fresh parsley, to serve

Instructions

Rinse an drain the canned white beans and put them in a blender together with the cashews, the lemon juice, and the nutritional yeast. If you want to make it a bit easier for your blender, you can soak them in water for 4-6 hours before using them. Put aside.

Heat some oil in a large pan and sauté the onion for about 3 minutes until they become translucent. After 2 minutes, add the garlic. Then add the spinach and cook for 3 more minutes. Season with salt and pepper. Add the artichokes and stir in the white bean cashew mixture.

Again season with salt, pepper, and if using red pepper flakes. Sprinkle with chopped fresh parsley and serve with whole wheat sesame crackers.

VEGAN PRETZEL GARLIC KNOTS

INGREDIENTS

2 cups all-purpose flour + more to dust the dough and surfaces

1 teaspoon instant yeast

1/3 teaspoon salt

1 pinch white sugar (make sure it's vegan!)

3/4 tablespoon olive oil + more to coat the dough

1/2 cup + 1 tablespoon water

Baking Soda Bath

3 cups water

1 1/2 tablespoons baking soda

Garlic Topping

1 garlic clove - minced

2 teaspoons olive oil

1/2 teaspoon dried oregano

1 teaspoon pretzel salt

INSTRUCTIONS

Combine the flour, instant yeast, salt, and white sugar in a mixing bowl. Add olive oil and water. Mix and knead by hand until a soft dough forms or put all the ingredients kitchen machine and let the machine knead the dough for you. If it's too sticky, you might want to add a few tablespoons more flour until the dough is non-sticky.

Drizzle the dough with more olive oil until coated. Let it sit, covered with a clean kitchen towel, in a warm spot until it doubles in size (about 2-3 hours - depending on the room temperature!).

Divide the dough into 10 equal parts, roll each part into a rope (about 6 inches / 15cm). Make a knot (check out the 2nd image of the post for visual instructions) and repeat for the rest.

Preheat the oven to 400°F/200°C.

Bring the water for the baking soda bath to a boil in a medium pot. Add the baking soda.

Cook each knot in the baking soda bath for about one minute. Transfer them onto a baking tray lined with parchment paper.

Mix the minced garlic, olive oil and dried oregano for the garlic topping. Brush the mixture onto the top of the Pretzel Knots. Sprinkle with pretzel salt.

Bake them in the oven for about 20 minutes until golden. They are absolutely delicious with my go-to vegan cheese sauce!

VEGAN CHICKEN NUGGETS

Ingredients

For the chickpea nuggets:

1/2 cup rolled oats

2 cups cooked chickpeas

1 small onion, chopped

1 teaspoon garlic powder

1 tablespoon nutritional yeast

1 teaspoon paprika powder

1 teaspoon salt

black pepper

1/2 teaspoon mustard (yellow mustard like Dijon or French's mustard)

3 tablespoons water

For the crust:

1/2 cup panko bread crumbs

1/2 cup cornflakes

1/2 cup almond milk

Instructions

Start by preparing the crust: Preheat the oven to 350 °F. Crumble the cornflakes with your hands in small pieces. Line a baking sheet with parchment paper and place the panko bread crumbs and cornflakes on top. Bake for about 2 minutes until golden-brown. Set aside.

In a small pan, heat some oil and sauté the onion for about 3 minutes. Set aside. Then place the oats into your food processor or blender and process into a fine flour. Add the rest of the ingredients (including the cooked onion) and pulse until you get a crumbly mixture.

Divide the chickpea mixture into 14 equal portions and form each portion into a nugget. Coat with some almond milk and roll in the baked panko bread crumbs and cornflakes.

Place on a new sheet of parchment paper and bake for 15 minutes.

Notes

If you have problems finding nutritional yeast, you can also just leave it out. This will slightly change the taste of the vegan chicken nuggets, but they will still be amazing!

Please not that the texture of these vegan chicken nuggets will be different from real chicken nuggets. The outside will be very crispy while the inside will be softer.

Make sure to leave some texture when you process the ingredients in your blender. Some of the chickpeas should still be partially intact.

I like to sauté the onions before adding them to the rest of the ingredients. If you don't do this they will still be a bit crispy, which I didn't like too much.

I like to use my blender to process the rolled oats into flour because it's much cheaper. But you will need to have a good blender to be able to do this. However, you could also use store-bought oat flour if you want.

VEGAN CHOCOLATE CARAMEL POPCORN

INGREDIENTS

For the popcorn

☐ 75g | 1/3 cup popcorn kernels

For the caramel

☐ 100g | 1/2 cup coconut sugar

☐ 2 tablespoons water

☐ 2 tablespoons coconut oil

☐ 2 tablespoons tahini

☐ 1/4 heaping teaspoon salt

For the chocolate drizzle

☐ 90g | 1/2 cup dairy free chocolate chips

INSTRUCTIONS

Warm a large heavy bottomed pan with a lid, over medium heat until hot. Pour in the popcorn kernels and put the lid on tightly. Move them around frequently by gently moving the pan. They will start popping after about 30 seconds.

Keep watching/listening until the popping stops then remove from the heat but keep the lid on in case a rogue kernel decides to surprise you!

Preheat oven to 300 degrees F

Add the coconut sugar and water to a small saucepan and warm over a medium heat until the sugar has dissolved and it is just starting the bubble.

Remove from the heat and add the coconut oil, tahini and salt. Stir really well until it is smooth. It is normal to see some pale flecks throughout. If lumps persist or it doesn't combine well put the pan back over a low heat and continue stirring. It will come together.

Remove the lid from the popcorn kernels and pour over the caramel. Be careful as it will be very hot. Stir until coated evenly.

Pour onto a baking tray lined with either a Silpat or baking parchment and spread out into a single layer. Put in the oven and bake for around 15 minutes until crunchy and golden.

Melt the chocolate chips over simmering water, or gently in a microwave, then drizzle over the popcorn with a spoon.

Place the tray in the fridge to allow the chocolate to set. If you are in a hurry you can put it in the freezer for 10 minutes. Once the chocolate is set break into pieces and store in an airtight container where it will keep well for a few days.

BLUEBERRY MUFFIN BITES

INGREDIENTS

1/4 cup (65g) nut/seed butter (I used SunButter)

1/4 cup (60g) applesauce

1/4 cup (80g) maple syrup

2/3 cup (70g) coconut flour

1/2 tsp salt

1 tsp vanilla extract

1 cup (150g) fresh blueberries*

INSTRUCTIONS

Preheat the oven to 375F.

Spread the blueberries on a pan lined with parchment paper and bake for 40-45 minutes.

Remove from the oven, cool for 10-15 minutes, then pull off the parchment paper and separate.

Whisk together the nut/seed butter, applesauce, maple syrup, and vanilla extract.

Stir in the coconut flour and salt.

Fold in the blueberries.

Roll into 12 balls.

Refrigerate until firm (3-4 hours).

Enjoy! Keep in the fridge

Baba Ganoush

Ingredients

2 medium eggplants

3 tablespoons extra virgin olive oil

2 cloves of garlic

3/4 teaspoon salt

1/4 cup tahini

3 tablespoons lemon juice

2 tablespoons chopped parsley

Instructions

Preheat the oven to 350 °F.

With a sharp knife, cut the eggplant into half lengthwise. Line a baking tray with parchment paper and place the eggplant halves on top with the flesh-side facing up.

Brush with olive oil (I used about one tablespoon in total).

Bake them for 40 minutes. Cover them with aluminium foil for the last 10-15 minutes, so they don't become too brown.

Let the eggplants cool down for about 10 minutes, so they are easier to handle. In the meanwhile place the remaining ingredients into a food processor.

Scrape out the flesh of the eggplant with a spoon and add it to the tahini mixture. Process until smooth.

Sprinkle with freshly chopped parsley, some more olive oil, and red pepper flakes. Serve with warm pita bread. Enjoy!

VEGAN PEANUT BUTTER BALLS

INGREDIENTS

1 cup (250g) Smooth Creamy Peanut Butter

1/3 cup (80ml) Vegan Whipped Cream*

2 cups (240g) Powdered Sugar

1 and 3/4 cups (300g) Vegan Chocolate or Vegan Chocolate Chips

1 tsp Coconut Oil

For Decoration (Optional):

Crushed Peanuts

INSTRUCTIONS

Add the peanut butter and powdered sugar to the mixing bowl and with the electric mixer on low speed mix it in. It will be crumbly.

Slowly add the vegan whipped cream until you achieve a thick consistency that you can easily roll into balls. You may not need to add all your whipped cream, it depends on the brand of peanut butter you're using, so go slow when you add in the whipped cream.

Roll the peanut butter mix into balls – aim to get 20 balls – and place them evenly on a parchment lined baking tray.

Place them into the freezer for a couple of hours until the balls have set solidly.

Place the vegan chocolate into a microwave safe dish. Microwave in 30-second intervals, bringing it out to stir every 30-seconds until your chocolate is melted. Add in the coconut oil and stir it in (makes the chocolate a little thinner and easier to work with).

Place each ball into the melted chocolate and use two teaspoons to cover it in chocolate and then lift it out and place it back onto the parchment lined baking tray. Sprinkle with crushed peanuts (optional).

When all the balls are covered in chocolate, place in the fridge for around 10 minutes for the chocolate to set.

Keep the balls stored in the fridge and serve directly from the fridge.

VEGAN ZA'ATAR CRACKERS

INGREDIENTS

1⅔ cup all-purpose flour

½ teaspoon baking powder

1/2 teaspoon salt

1 teaspoon olive oil

1/2 cup water + 1 tablespoon water for brushing the top

1 teaspoon maple syrup

1 tablespoon za'atar seasoning

INSTRUCTIONS

Preheat the oven to 400°F/200°C.

In a mixing bowl add in the flour, baking powder, and salt, whisk and then add in the olive oil and water. Mix with a large wooden spoon until it comes together and knead with your hand until it's a smooth dough. Add more flour if the dough is too sticky.

On a lightly floured parchment paper, roll out the dough as thin and even as possible. Use more flour if you need to.

Mix 1 tablespoon of water with 1 teaspoon of maple syrup and brush the top of the crackers with it. Then sprinkle the za'atar seasoning on top.

Cut it with a pizza cutter length- and widthwise into individual crackers. Carefully pull the parchment paper with the crackers onto a baking sheet.

Bake them in the oven for about 15 minutes until they get crispy and golden brown. Let them cool off a bit before digging in. They're delicious with homemade hummus.

Vegan Ranch

Ingredients

1 cup vegan mayonnaise

1 teaspoon garlic powder

1 teaspoon onion powder

2 tablespoons chopped parsley

2 tablespoons chopped dill

1 tablespoon chives

1 teaspoon apple cider vinegar

2 tablespoons unsweetened plant-based milk

1/4 teaspoon paprika powder (optional)

salt, to taste

black pepper, to taste

Instructions

Combine all ingredients in a bowl and stir until well combined.

Notes

You can serve the vegan ranch with veggie sticks, as a salad dressing, with cauliflower wings, on a veggie burger, or with vegan chicken nuggets. Or drizzle it over pizza!

Always make sure the plant-based milk you use is unsweetened.

If you're using the vegan ranch as a dressing for salad, I recommend adding more plant-based milk.

For a lighter version you can use plant-based yogurt (again, make sure it's unsweetened) or silken tofu instead of vegan mayonnaise.

Stored in an airtight container in the fridge, this recipe will last up to 7 days in the fridge.

NUT-FREE GRANOLA BARS (VEGAN AND GLUTEN-FREE)

INGREDIENTS

3 tablespoons (18g) ground flaxseed (I used golden) mixed with 6 tablespoons water

1/2 cup (68g) raw, unsalted sunflower seed kernels, ground (without the shells)

1 cup (100g) QUICK/INSTANT cooking oats (NOT regualr, see NOTE)

1/2 cup (64g) superfine oat flour

2 teaspoons ground cinnamon

2 teaspoons ground ginger (see NOTE)

1/4 teaspoon fine salt

1/4 cup + 2 tablespoons (120g) pure maple syrup

1/3 cup (75g) dairy-free semi-sweet chocolate chips

INSTRUCTIONS

Preheat the oven to 350°F (177°C) and line a square baking dish with parchment paper cut to fit and lay both directions. My baking dish is is a little smaller than 8x8, more like 7 1/2, so if yours is a true 8x8, the bars just will be a bit thinner on the edges.

In a small bowl, mix the flaxseed and 6 tablespoons of water and heat in the microwave for 30 seconds. Whisk well and set aside.

To a food processor, add the sunflower kernels and process about 30-45 seconds until a fine flour forms (as in the photo). Be careful not to over process or it will start to turn into a paste.

To a large bowl, add all of the sunflower flour to it, along with the oats, oat flour, cinnamon, ginger and salt. Stir really well. Add the chocolate chips.

To the bowl of reserved flaxseed mixture, it should be thick, whisk in the syrup well. Make sure it is no longer warm before adding to the dry ingredients (so it doesn't melt the chocolate chips). Stir everything together for a good minute or so until it all comes together in a moist, sticky batter. The more you stir, the stickier it will get. This is good, as that flaxseed helps to bind the bars.

To the lined pan, add the batter and spread out evenly with the back of the spoon as best you can. Now, take a square piece of parchment paper the size of the pan and place it on top. Press the mixture down flat and smooth out the top. Smooth your fingers along the edges and corners, making sure it's even. Really BE PA-TIENT with this step ensuring you are properly spreading it out to the corners and along the edges. Do not sloppily or quickly press it down or the bars will not form properly when baking.

Once it's smooth, flat and even, top with extra chocolate chips if desired. Bake for 30-32 minutes until the edges are looking golden brown and the middle is firm to the touch

Roasted Chickpeas

Ingredients

2 cans chickpeas

2 tablespoons olive oil

1 teaspoon smoked paprika powder

1 teaspoon garlic powder

1/2 teaspoon salt

Instructions

Drain the canned chickpeas. Then dry them really well using a clean dishtowel. Just gently roll them between the dishtowel. You could also use paper towel.

In a medium bowl, toss the chickpeas with olive oil. We'll add the spices after baking because they have a tendency to burn. So don't worry about them for now.

Preheat your oven to 350 °F. Line a baking sheet with parchment paper. Spread the chickpeas on the baking sheet and bake for 25 minutes.

Then take the chickpeas out of the oven and place them in the bowl you used before. Add the spices and toss well until the chickpeas are coated evenly.

Return them to the baking sheet and bake for another 10 minutes until they're browned and crunchy.

HOMEMADE GLUTEN-FREE + VEGAN GOLDFISH (ALLERGY-FREE, GRAIN-FREE)

ingredients

1 Cup Chickpea Flour

3 TB Nutritional Yeast

2 Tsp Olive Oil

1 Tsp Baking Powder

1/4 Tsp Onion Powder

1/4 Tsp Turmeric

1/8 Tsp Paprika (optional)

1/4 Cup Water

instructions

Preheat the oven to 400°F.

In a mixing bowl, combine all ingredients except the water and whisk together.

Now slowly add the water (you may need more or less) until you mix and get a rollable dough.

Now roll the dough out between 2 Silpats (or parchment paper) to 1/4 inch thick.

Use a little fish cookie cutter and cut, re-roll if needed, and cut again, until you have as many fish as you can make.

Use a toothpick to make a small eye and smile line on the surface of the fish.

Place the goldfish on a greased lined baking sheet and bake the goldfish in the oven for about 10 minutes.

CRISPY BAKED MAC AND CHEESE BALLS (VEGAN + GLUTEN FREE)

INGREDIENTS

Cheese sauce:

2 ½ cups cooked potato (about 2-3 medium potatoes, see note)

½ cup cooked sweet or yellow onion (about ½ a medium onion)

5 tablespoons cooked carrots (about 5-6 baby carrots or one large carrot)

1/4 cup cooked yellow pepper (about 1/3 of a whole medium pepper)

4 cloves garlic

1 ½ cups raw cashews (see note, I use NOW Foods brand)

½ cup unsweetened cashew milk

4 teaspoons apple cider vinegar

2-3 teaspoons sea salt (see note)

1/8 teaspoon ground mustard

Crispy coating:

¾ cup cornmeal

¾ cup breadcrumbs (gluten-free if needed)

½ cup hemp seeds

1 ½ teaspoons sea salt (may need an extra 1/2 teaspoon depending on preference)

Extras:

2 cups unsweetened cashew milk

8 ounces macaroni pasta (I use Living Now Quinoa Macaroni Pasta)

INSTRUCTIONS

To cook the veggies, I boil potato, onion, carrots and yellow pepper together in a pot of water until soft.

Make cheese sauce:

Once cooked, place the veggies into a high speed blender with the garlic, cashews, milk, vinegar, 2 teaspoons salt, and ground mustard.

Blend on high using the blenders tamper tool to help mix the ingredients around. It will be thick and hard to get going but the tamper tool will help and eventually everything will blend smooth.

Take out 1 ½ cups for drizzle and dipping, then add the last teaspoon salt and blend again.

Make balls:

Cook pasta according to package directions, but cook al dente (I cooked 2 minutes less than the package said).

Combine the sauce left in the blender and the cooked pasta in a large bowl. Mix well.

Drop spoonfuls, about 2-3 inches big, onto a parchment lined cookie sheet, making them as round as possible.

Chill for at least an hour, 2-3 is better. You want the pasta balls easy to handle and not falling apart.

Meanwhile, combine the cornmeal, breadcrumbs, hemp seeds and salt in a food processor and pulse to incorporate to make crispy coating. Place mixture into a bowl. You can also simply mix in a bowl but you wont have ground hemp seeds.

Once the mac and cheese balls are chilled, preheat the oven to 400 F (200 C).

Carefully pick up the parchment paper with the chilled balls on it and move it to the counter, then line the cookie sheet with more parchment paper. You can also simply line another cookie sheet if you're too nervous to move the one with the balls on it.

Put the two cups of milk in a bowl. Dip each mac and cheese ball in the milk, then into the bowl of crispy coating. I use one hand to dip into the milk, then put it in the crispy coating where I use my other hand to cover it well and then place on the clean parchment lined cookie sheet. This avoids clumpy wet coating.

Once done, bake for 20-25 minutes or until the crispy coating just begins to crisp.

Then broil for 1-2 minutes until browned. Do not overbake or you will lose the creamy cheesy inside.

Devour smothered in more cheesy sauce, careful not to burn your mouth. This will not be easy as it will be very tempting to grab them from the cookie sheet and shove into your mouth.

SPICY OIL-FREE MEXICAN HUMMUS

Ingredients

1 15 ounce can of chickpeas – drained and rinsed well

2 cloves of garlic – blanched

1 jalapeno pepper – seeded

1 tablespoon of chili powder

1 teaspoon of cumin

1 teaspoon of finely ground sea salt

1/4 cup of seeded and chopped tomato

1/2 cup of water

Instructions

Boil two cups of water in a small sauce pan and add the garlic cloves. Turn off the heat and let the garlic sit for two minutes. Remove the garlic and put in the food processor.

Add the chickpeas, jalapeno, chili powder, cumin, salt, and tomato and begin processing. SLOWLY add the water. When the hummus is thick and creamy stop adding the water.

Pea Hummus

Ingredients

400 g (15 oz) can of chickpeas - not yet drained (garbanzo beans)

150 g (1 cup) fresh or frozen peas

2 tbsp tahini

2 tsp lemon juice

1 clove of garlic minced

Pinch of salt and pepper

Instructions

Drain the chickpeas over a bowl to collect the liquid (aquafaba), then add the chickpeas to a blender or food processor.

Run the frozen peas under hot water to thaw, then also add them to the blender, along with the tahini, lemon juice, garlic salt and pepper as well as 4 tbsp of the aquafaba.

Blend for a few minutes until thick and creamy. You may need to scrape the sides down periodically. Add a little more aquafaba if necessary to get it a thick and creamy consistency.

tropical cashew no bake snack bars {paleo}

INGREDIENTS

For the Bars:

1 1/4 cup dried pineapple

1 cup raw cashews

1/3 cup pumpkin seeds

1/2 cup shredded unsweetened coconut

1/4 cup sunflower seed butter or other creamy no stir nut butter of choice.

1 tsp vanilla

parchment paper for 8×8 pan.

For the Frosting/Coconut Icing:

1/2 cup coconut butter/oil

1 tbsp maple syrup

Lime juice

Lime Slices

INSTRUCTIONS

Line an 8×8 inch square pan with parchment paper. Set aside.

In a blender or food processor, blend together 1 1/4 cup dried pineapple, 1 cup cashews, 1/3 cup pumpkin seeds, 1/2 cup of your coconut. You might have to scrape down sides a few times.

Next Add in your 1/4 cup sunflower seed nut butter (or other smooth nut butter of choice), vanilla, and blend again until batter is combined and starting to stick together.

Press batter into 8×8 pan.

Finally, make the frosting/icing for the top.

Blend 1 tbsp lime juice, 1 – 2 tbsp maple syrup, and softened coconut oil or butter until smooth. Spread over bars. Place in fridge to chill for 30 minutes.

Remove from fridge and slice into squares.

Drizzle a little maple syrup on top. Then a sprinkle of shredded unsweetened coconut. Add a slice of lime on top of each bar.

Keep bars in fridge. They will be fine at room temperature for 1 hour or so before the icing starts to melt. Freezer friendly.

WATERMELON PIZZA

Ingredients

1 watermelon

1 cup coconut yogurt (or greek yogurt for non-vegan)

1/2 cup strawberries, sliced in half

1/2 cup raspberries

1/2 cup cherries

1/2 cup blueberries

1/2 cup pomegranate seeds

honey or maple syrup (optional)

Instructions

Using a sharp knife, cut off a slice of watermelon right down the middle, about 2-3 inches thick.

Using a spatula, spread an even layer of your yogurt around the watermelon leaving a bit of empty space at the top. (where your "pizza crust" is.)

Layer your fresh fruit on top as you please. You can add as little or as many toppings as you like!

Drizzle with honey or maple syrup for a little extra sweetness if desired.

PAN FRIED CINNAMON BANANAS

INGREDIENTS

☐ 2 bananas Slightly Overripe

☐ 2 tablespoons sugar (you can substitute granulated Splenda, if you like)

☐ 1 teaspoon cinnamon

☐ 1/4 teaspoon nutmeg (optional)

INSTRUCTIONS

Slice the bananas into rounds, approximately 1/3 inch thick.

In a small bowl, combine the sugar, cinnamon, and nutmeg (if desired). Set aside.

Lightly spray a large skillet with nonstick oil spray. Warm over medium heat.

Add the banana rounds and sprinkle 1/2 of the cinnamon mixture on top.

Cook for about 2-3 minutes.

Flip the rounds, sprinkle with the remaining cinnamon mixture

Cook for 2-3 more minutes until the bananas are soft and warmed through.

PEANUT BUTTER JELLY APPLE NACHOS

Ingredients

1 large apple (or 2 small apples), I used pink lady

1-2 tablespoons smooth peanut butter, melted

1-2 tablespoons jelly, your favorite flavor

chia seeds, optional

Instructions

Cut apple(s) in thin slices and arrange on a plate.

Top with melted peanut butter and jelly.

Option to top with a sprinkle of chia seeds or nuts.

Enjoy!

Healthy 3 Ingredient Pumpkin Cake Pops

Ingredients

1 cup coconut flour sifted

1/2-3/4 cup pumpkin puree not pumpkin pie filling*

1/4 cup granulated sweetener of choice I used coconut palm

sugar

Cinnamon to taste optional

1/4 cup dairy free chocolate chips optional**

Instructions

Preheat the oven to 350 and grease a large cookie sheet or baking tray and set aside.

In a large mixing bowl, combine the coconut flour, pumpkin puree, granulated sweetener and cinnamon mix well. If using chocolate chips, mix those in until fully incorporated.

Using your hands, shape into small balls and place on the greased cookie sheet. Depending on the texture you want, bake for around 10 minutes (for a softer cake texture) or up to 15 minutes (very dense and crumbly). Remove from oven and allow to cool completely before eating.

10-MINUTE EASY VEGAN PISTACHIO GRANOLA

Ingredients

1 cup roasted unsalted shelled pistachios

1/2 cup old-fashioned rolled oats

2 tablespoons pure maple syrup

1 tablespoon virgin coconut oil, melted

1/4 teaspoon ground cinnamon

1/8 to 1/4 teaspoon fine sea salt, to taste

Instructions

Preheat the oven to 350F. Line a small baking tray with parchment paper.

Meanwhile, add all the granola ingredients to a medium mixing bowl and toss, ensuring every last bit is thoroughly coated.

Spread the mixture into an even layer in the lined tray.

Bake for 8 minutes, or until wafting a rich toasted scent and the pistachios are light golden-brown with just the slightest sheen to them. The granola will firm and crisp as it cools, so go on look and scent rather than touch.

Let cool completely on the tray.

Serve with a splash of almond milk or sprinkle over a bowl of coconut yogurt.

Store at room temperature in an airtight glass jar until ready to assemble.

TURMERIC SNACK BITESTurmeric Snack Bites in a bowl with turmeric powder

INGREDIENTS

1/2 cup | 70 grams walnuts

1/2 cup | 70 grams unsweetened desiccated/shredded coconut

1 cup | about 8 pitted medjool dates, roughly chopped

1 teaspoon ground tumeric

1/2 teaspoon ground cinnamon

1 tablespoon unsweetened cocoa powder

INSTRUCTIONS

Add all of your ingredients to a high powdered blender or food processor and pulse until the dates and walnuts are broken up into small pieces and the mixture sticks together. If your mixture is too dry add a couple more dates. You may need to stop to scrape the sides down occasionally.

Transfer the mixture to a small bowl for easier rolling. Scoop out 1 tablespoon of the mixture at a time and roll into little balls.

Store these in the fridge for up to a week.

10 Minute Salted Almond + Honey Snack Bites

Ingredients

1 cup raw almonds (unsalted)

1 cup large flake oats

1/3 cup almond butter

1/3 cup raw honey

1/2 tsp vanilla extract

1/4 tsp sea salt

1/4 tsp sesame seeds (optional, you can get creative with your fave topping)

Melted dark chocolate for drizzling (optional but very recommended ��)

Method

In a food processor, add the almonds and oats. Pulse for 20-30 seconds until it becomes the texture of coarse breadcrumbs.

Pour into a large bowl and add the honey, almond butter, vanilla extract and sea salt.

Using a spatula, mix thoroughly to combine until a thick dough forms. If its too wet, add a sprinkle of oats and stir.

Using damp hands, roll into 8-10 balls and roll into sesame seeds. Move into the fridge or freezer to set for 15 minute.

Drizzle with melted chocolate if desired!

HEALTHY VEGAN CHOCOLATE CHIP COOKIE DOUGH

INGREDIENTS

Caution: the scale button does not work for values in parenthesis.

2 cups (400g) cooked chickpeas, drained

1/3 cup (80 ml) coconut oil, melted and slightly cooled

1/4 cup (60 ml) maple syrup

2 teaspoon vanilla extract

1/2 teaspoon sea salt*

3 Tablespoons (45g) coconut flour

1/2 cup (75g) mini chocolate chips**

INSTRUCTIONS

In a food processor, blend the chickpeas until smooth.

Add oil, maple syrup, vanilla, and sea salt. Blend again for about one minute, until creamy.

Add coconut flour, blend, scrape sides, and blend again.

Fold in the mini chocolate chips and stir well with a small rubber spatula.

Transfer the dough in a large serving bowl and chill for 2 hours in the refrigerator.

Serve the bowl of cookie dough like you would do with hummus, with graham crackers for dipping, or simply spoon the cookie dough and serve with vanilla ice cream.